HANDBAGS

Coloring Book

THIS BOOK BELONGS TO: ______________________

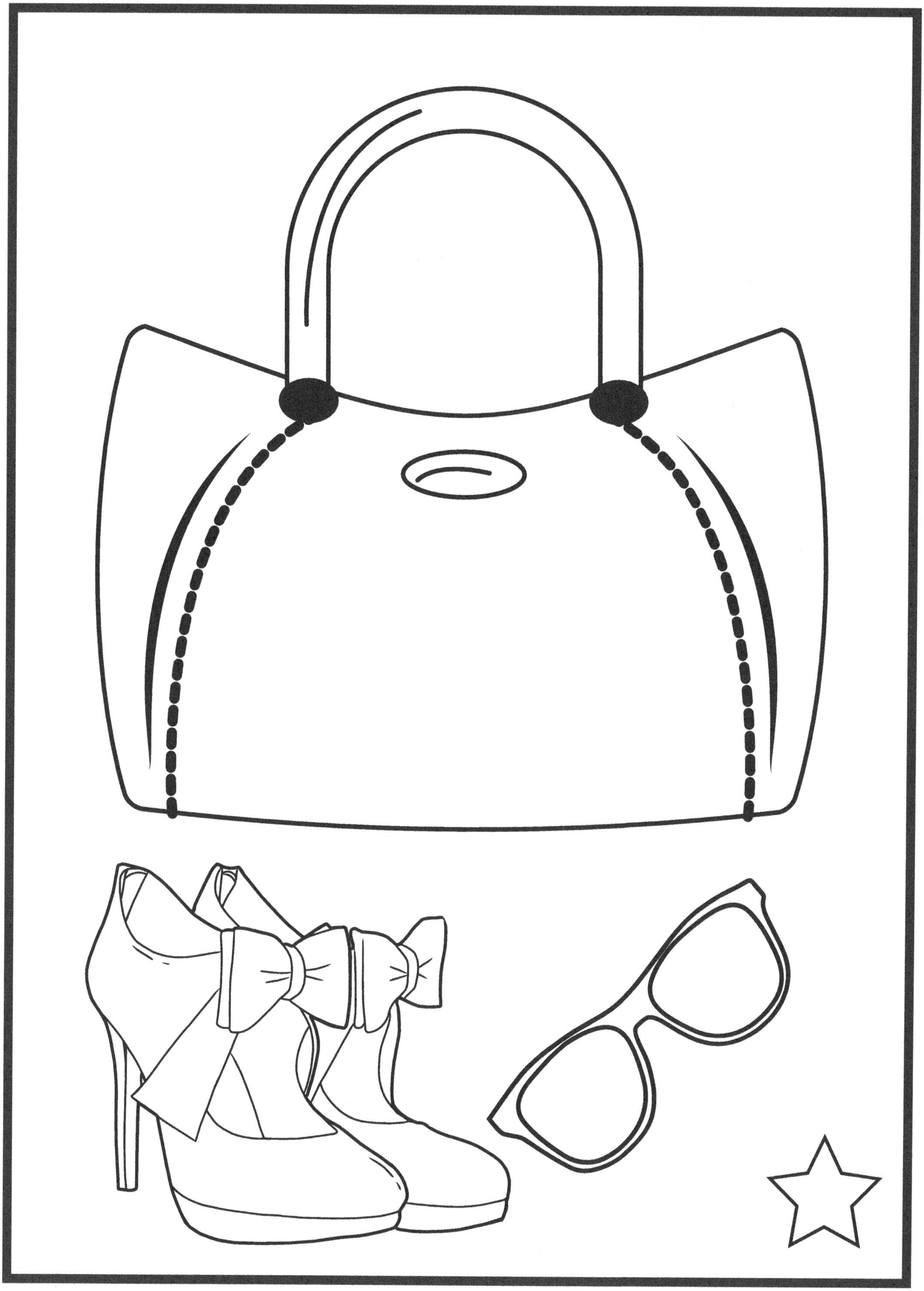

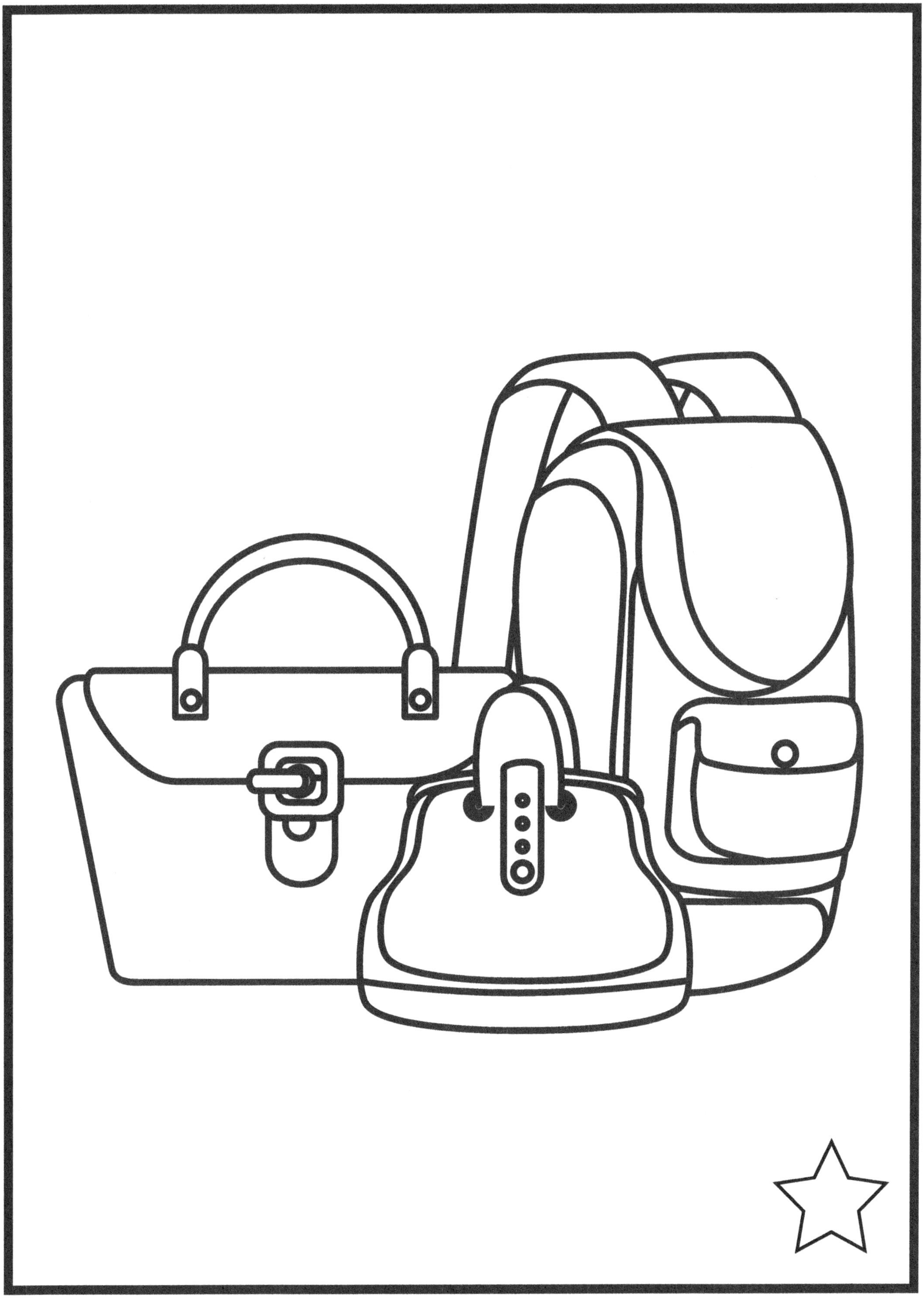

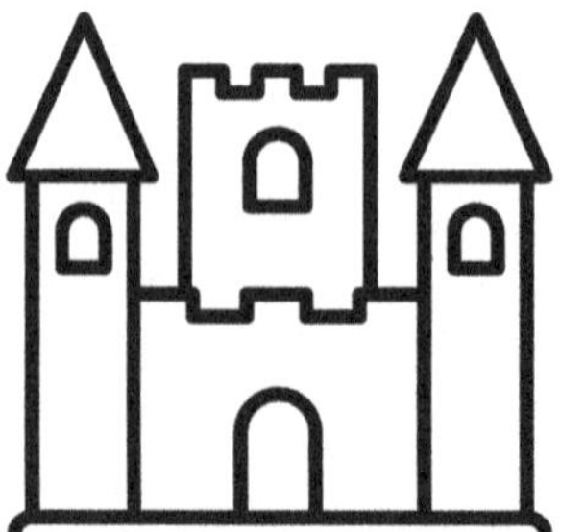

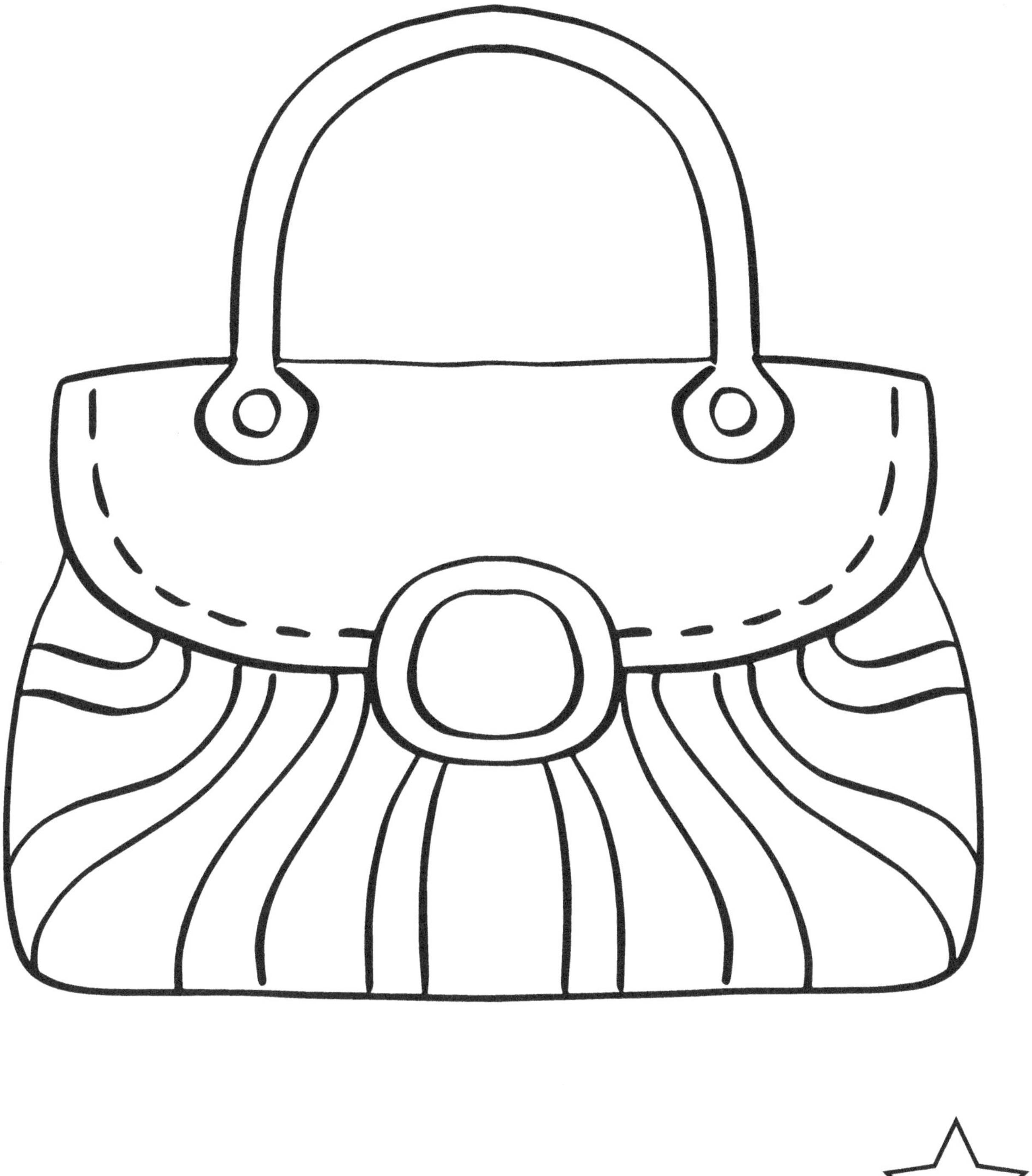

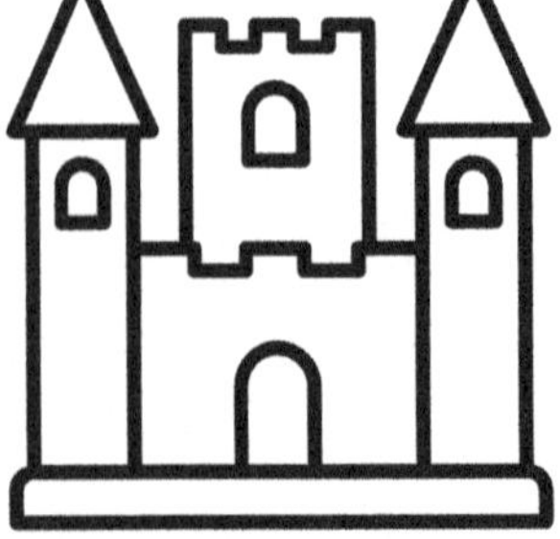

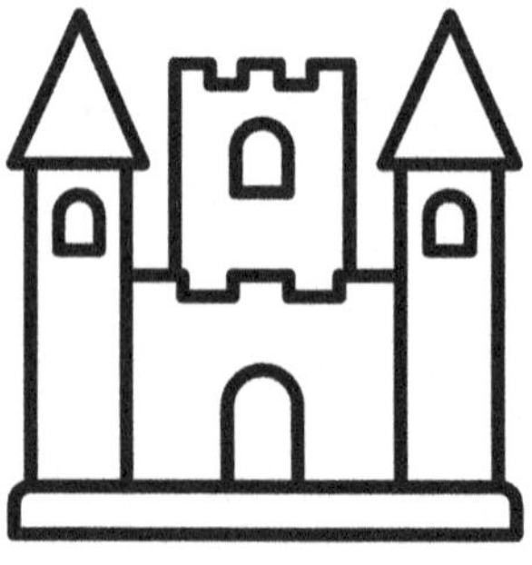

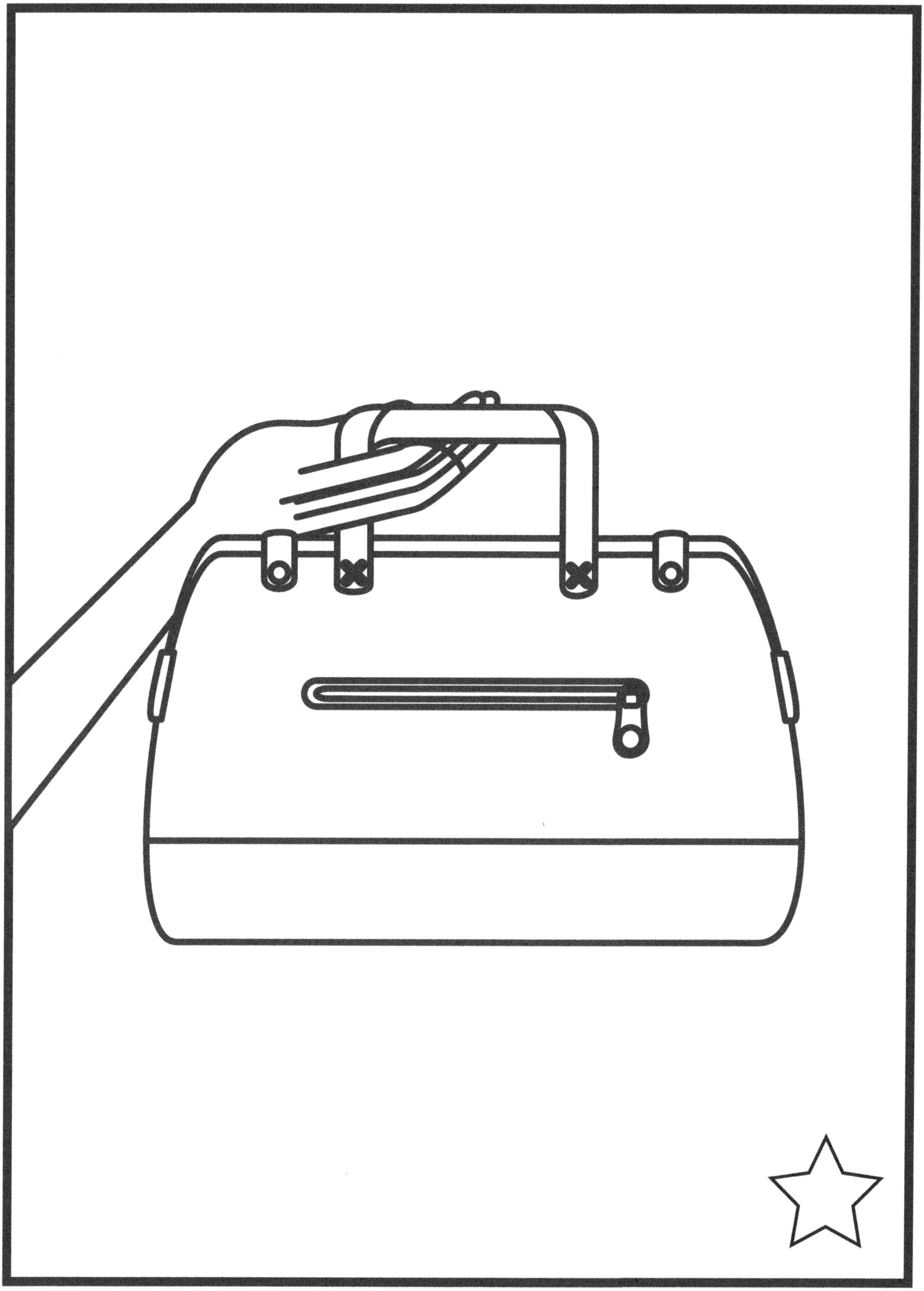

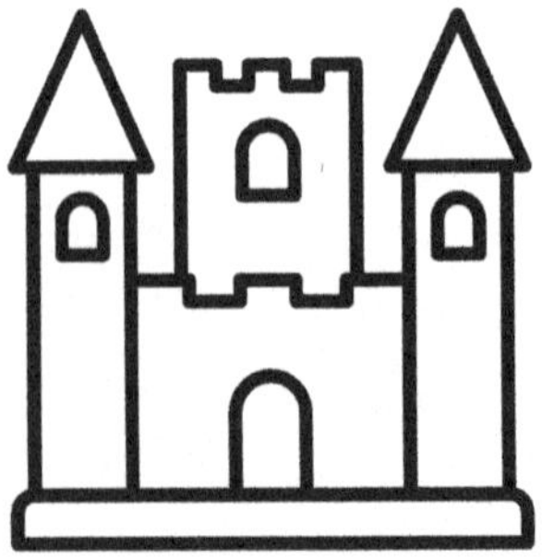

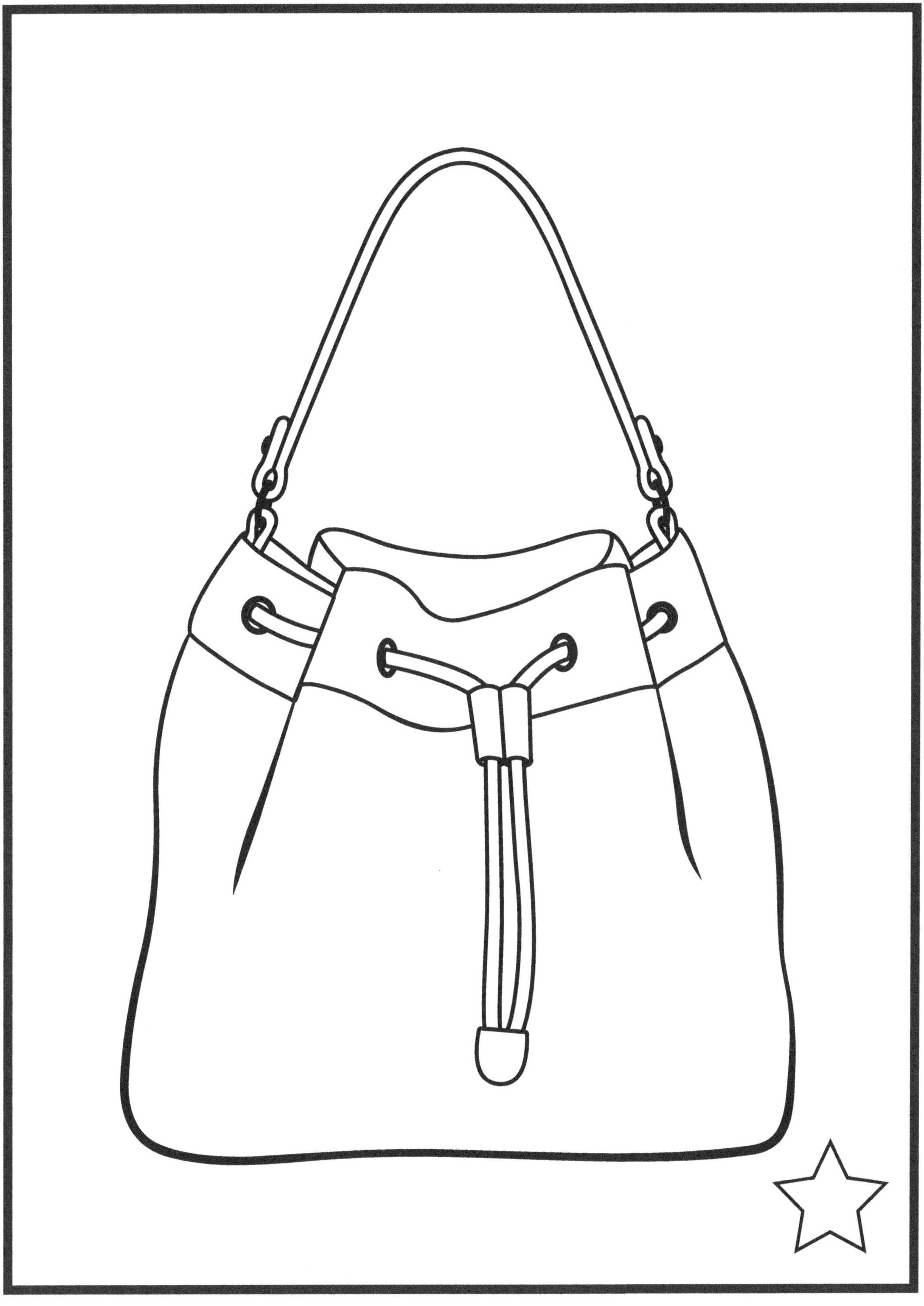

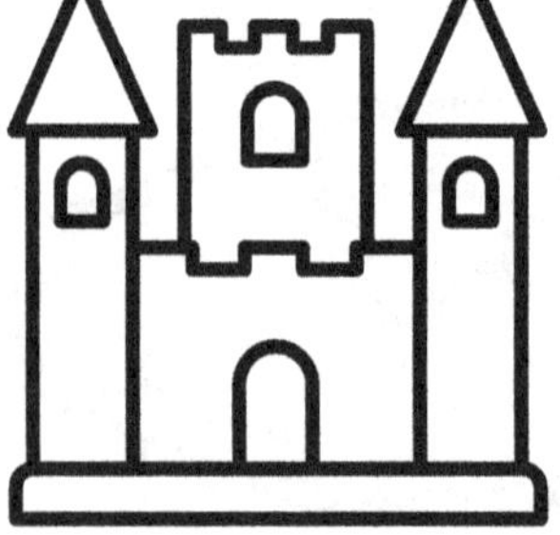

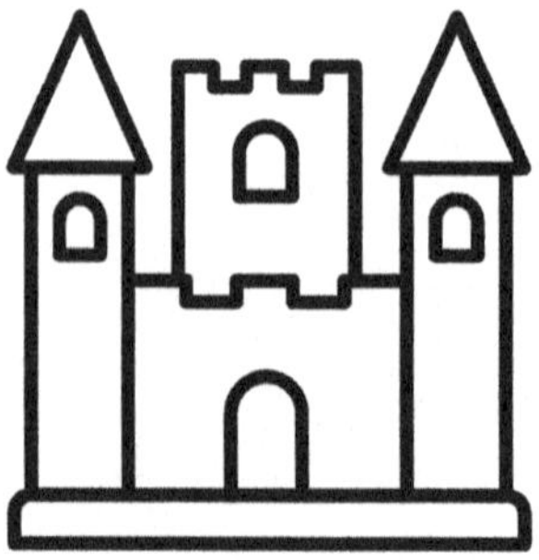

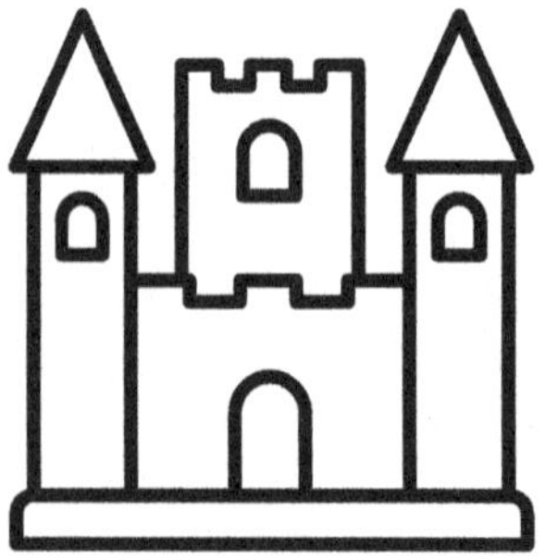

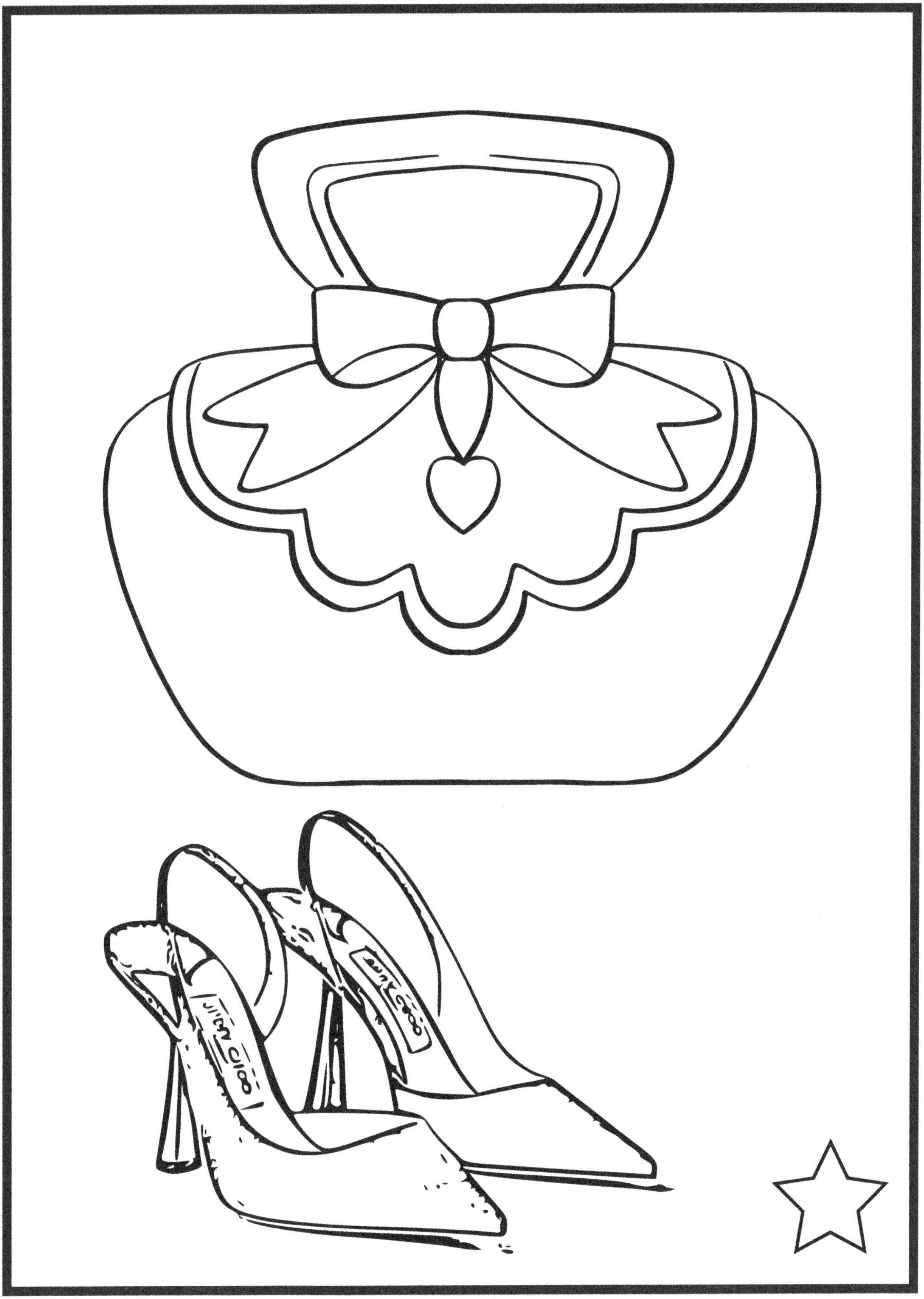

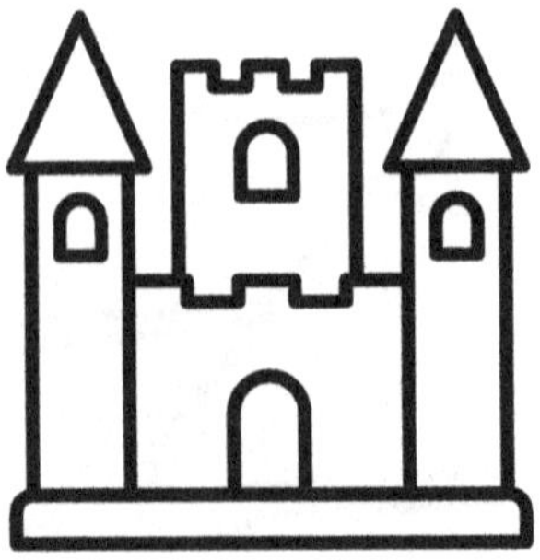

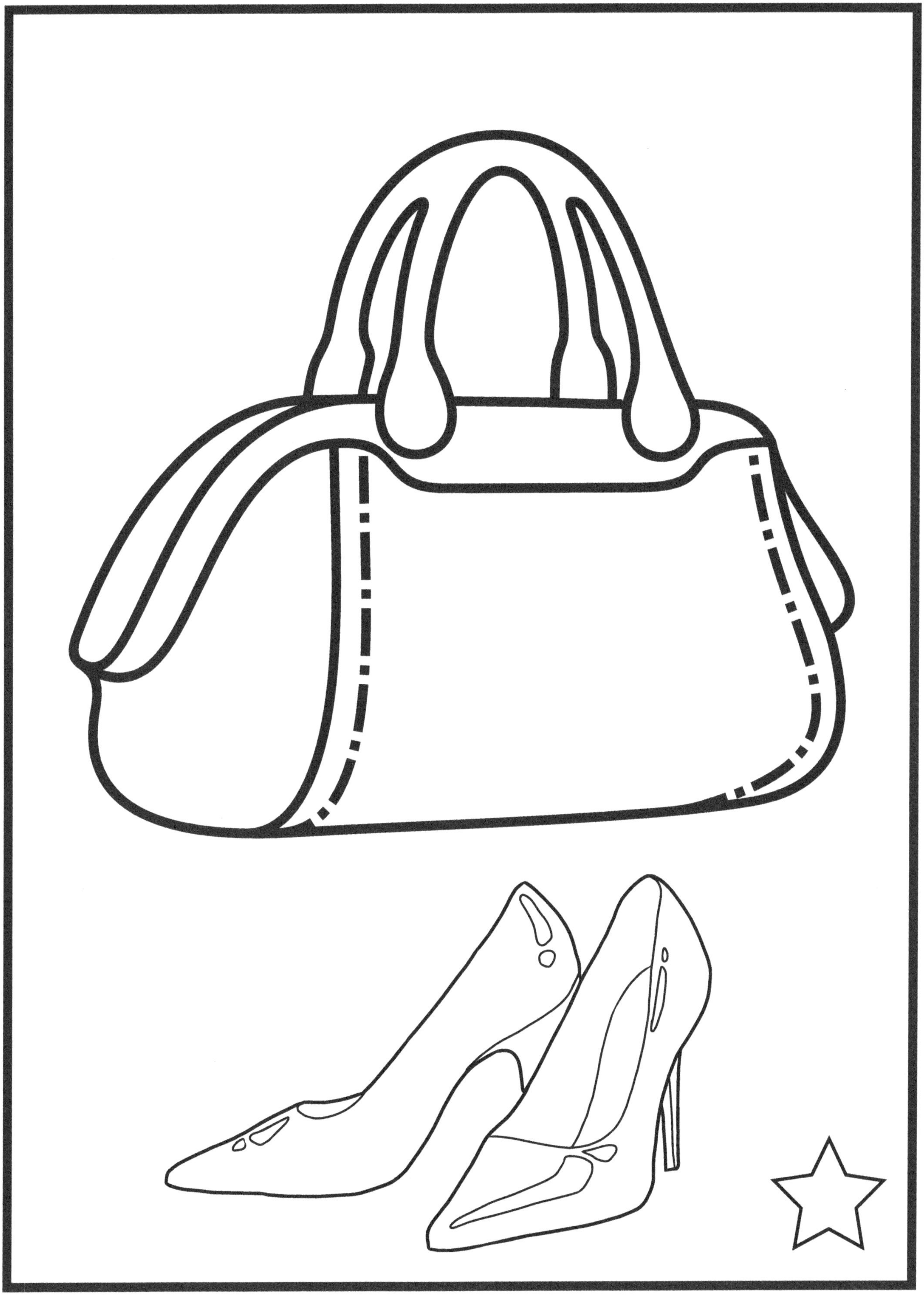

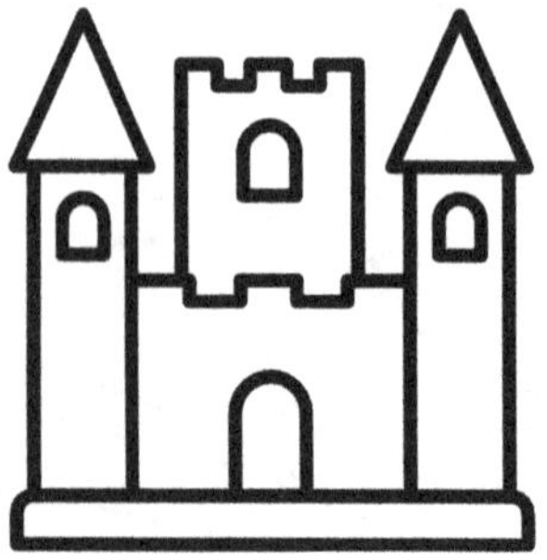

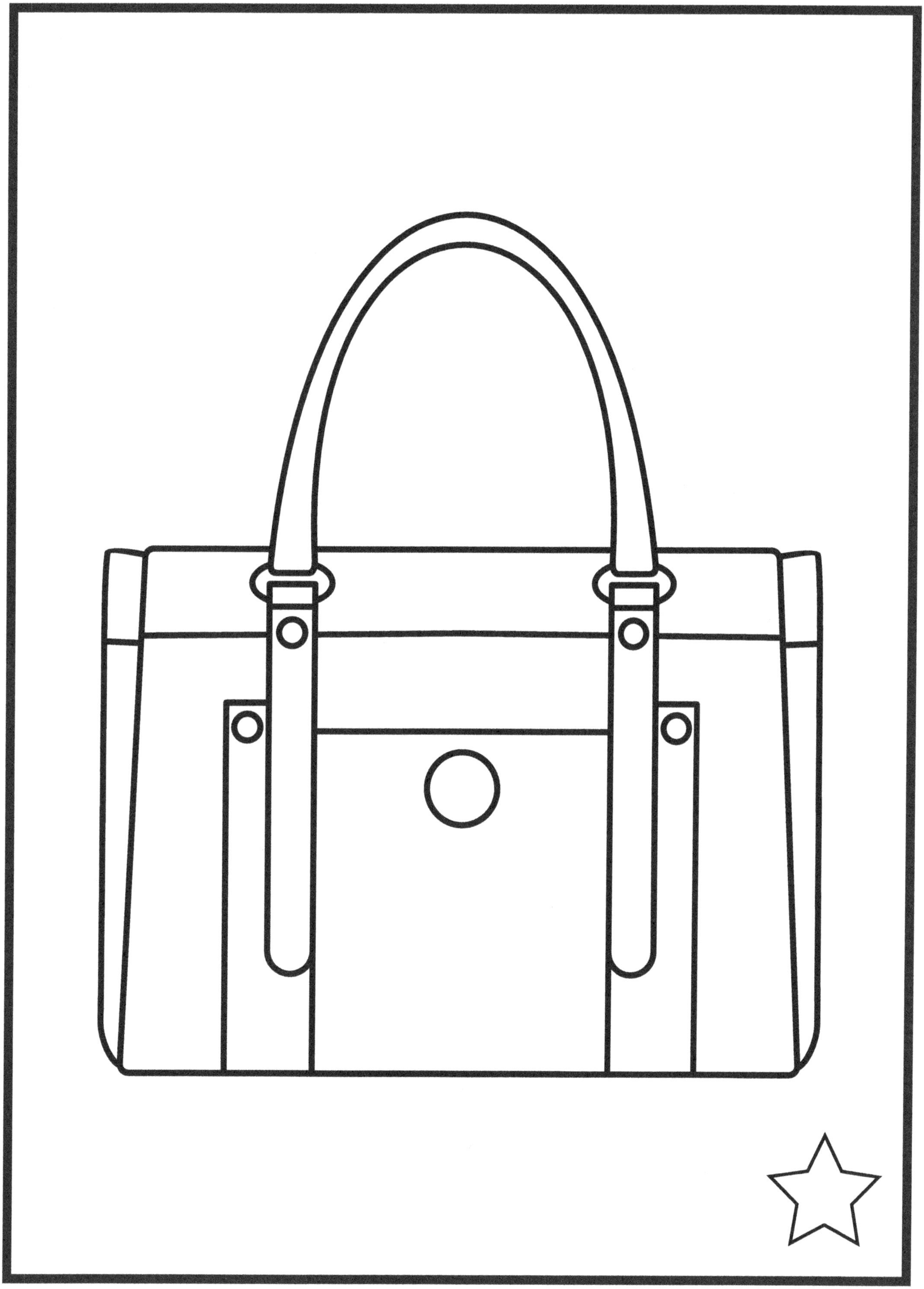

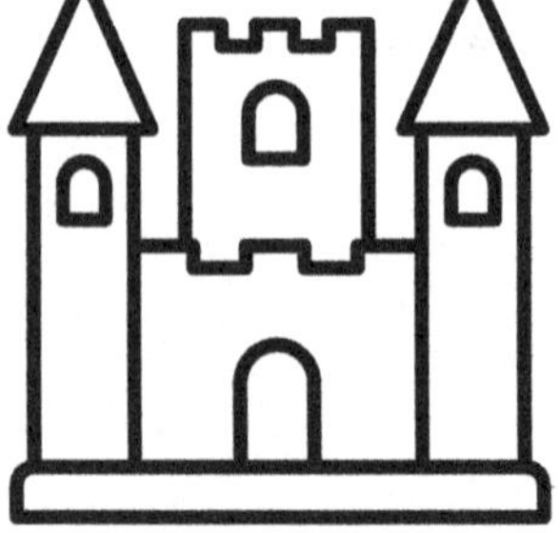

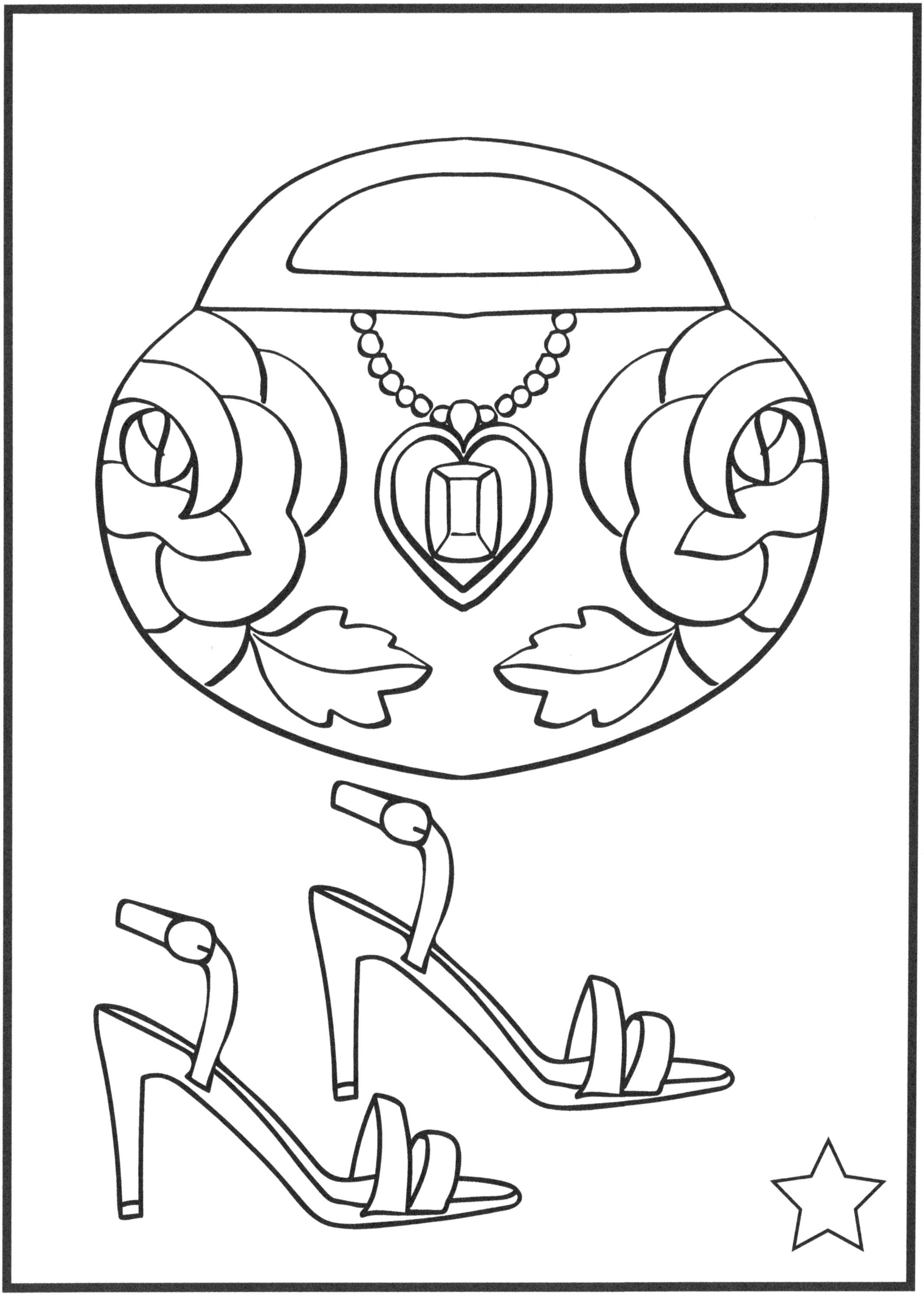

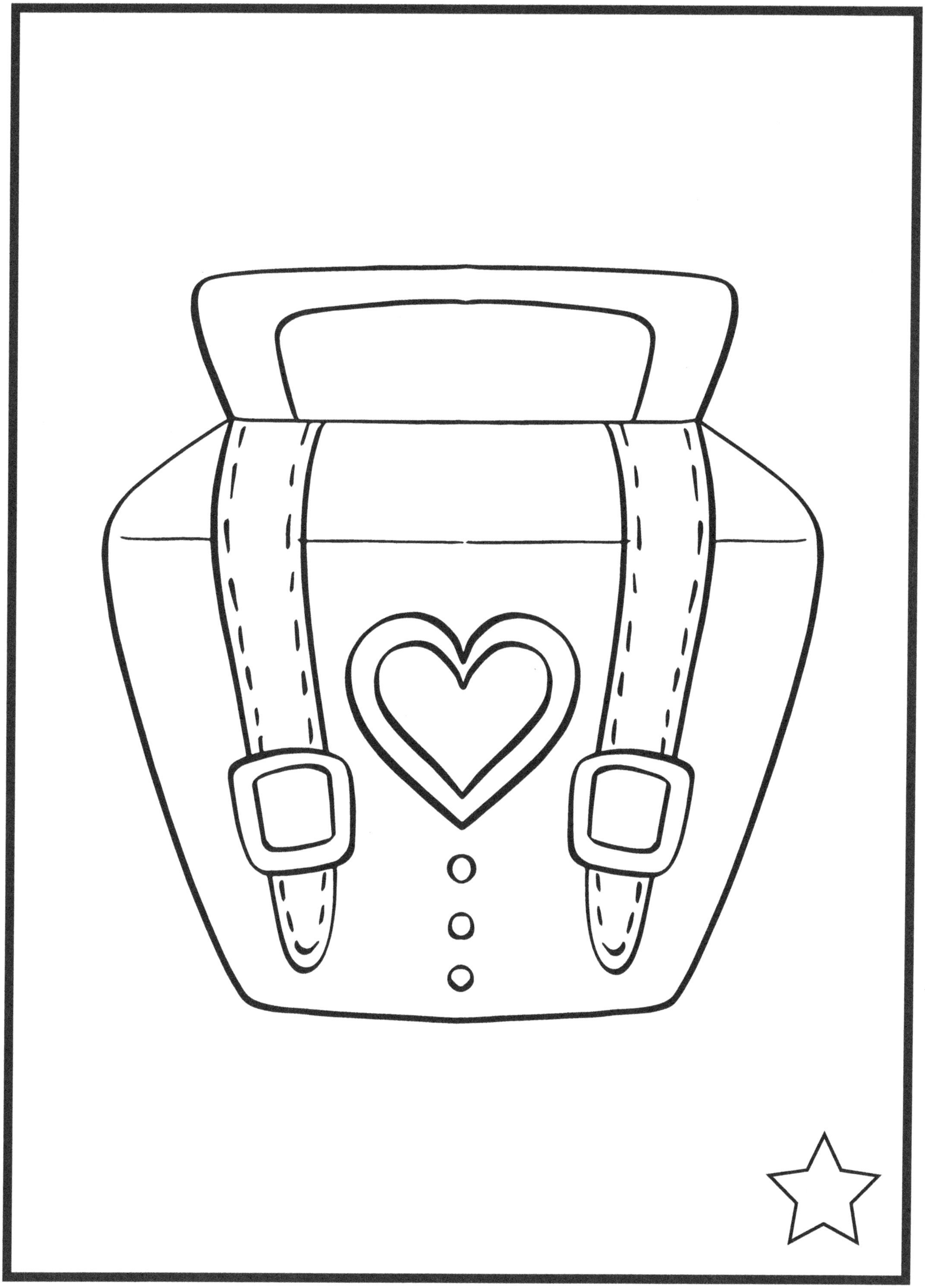

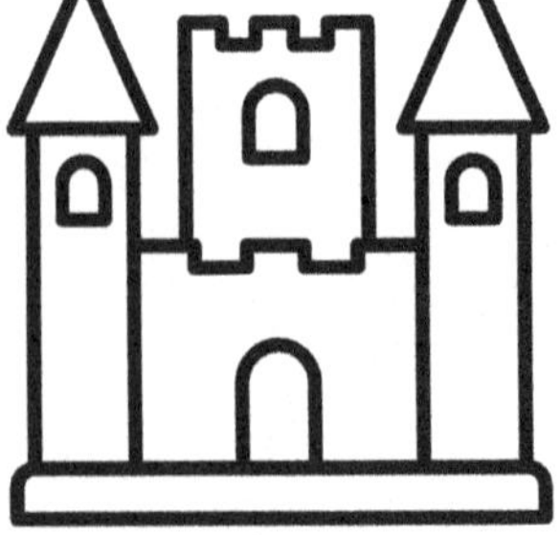

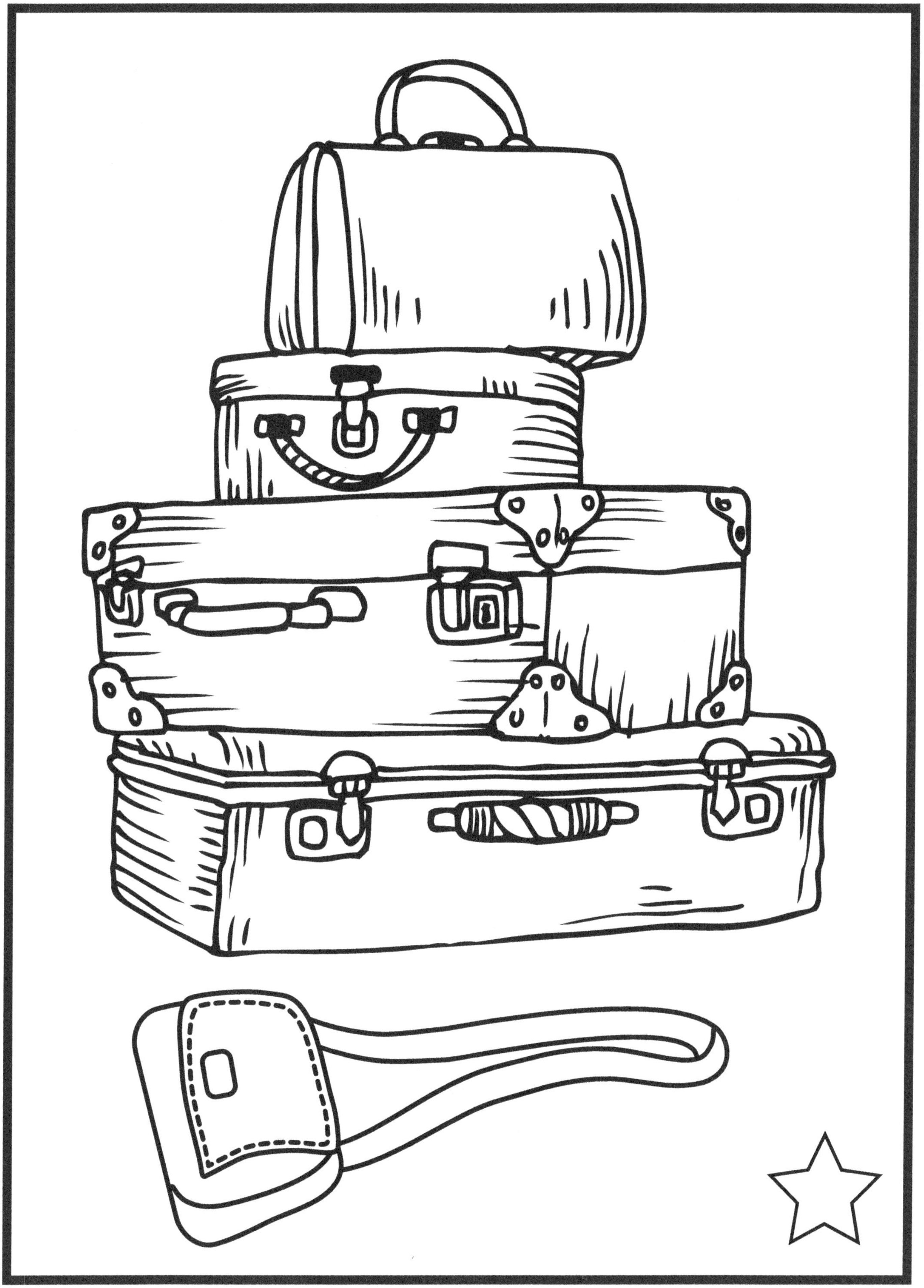

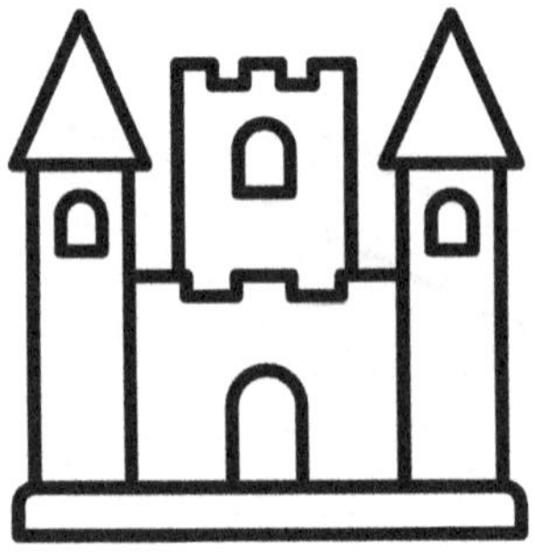

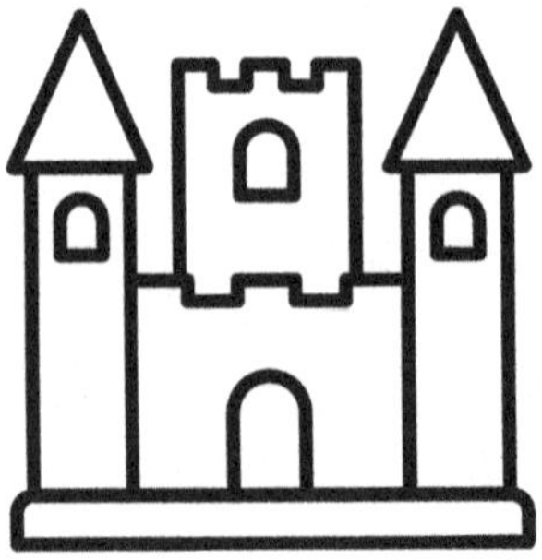

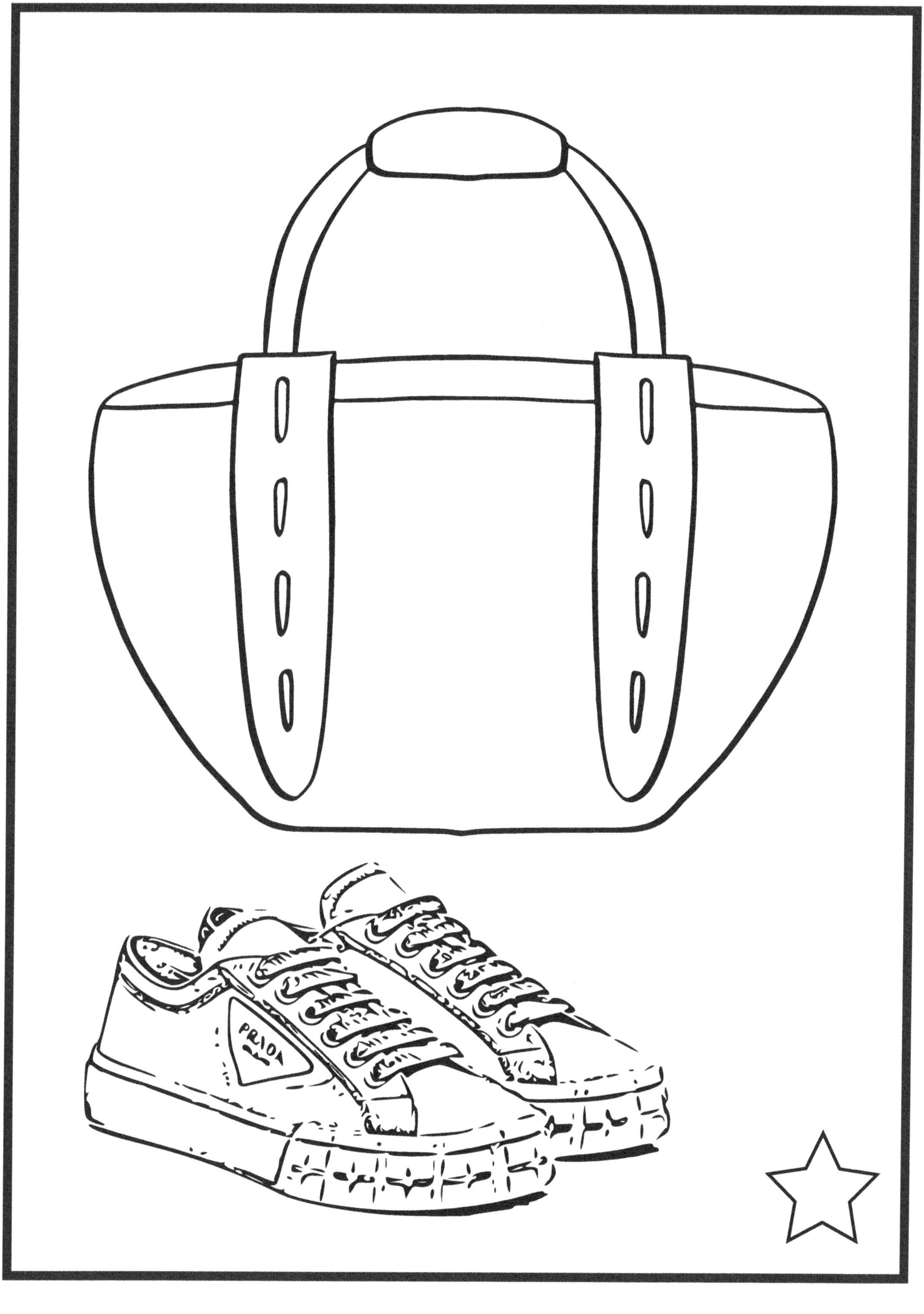
PRADA

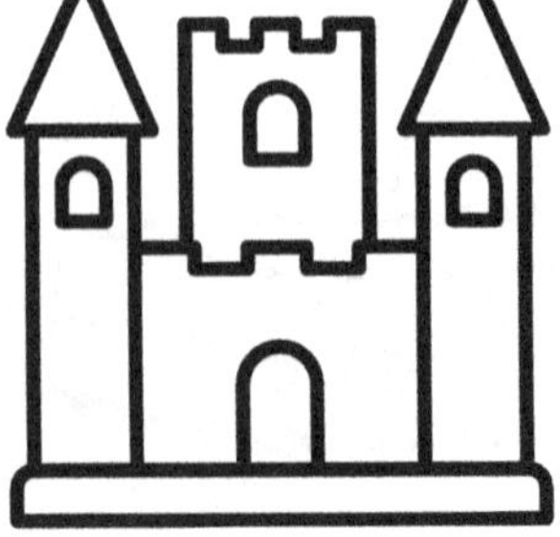

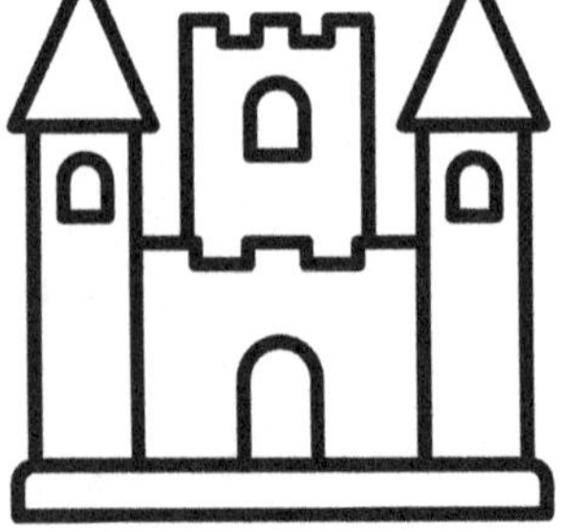

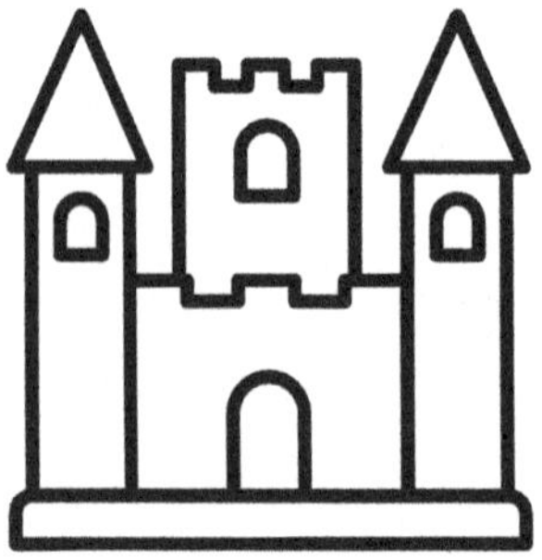

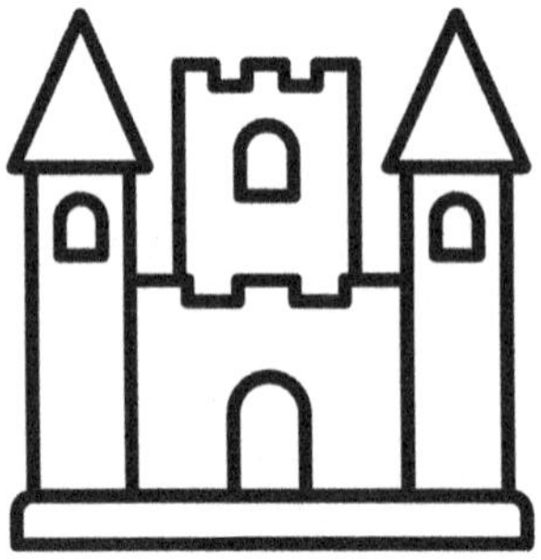

Made in United States
Orlando, FL
01 March 2023

30567078R00037